S0-ASG-107

A Grateful Nation Celebrates

Those Who
SERVE

FAMILY
CHRISTIAN
PRESS

A Grateful Nation Celebrates

Those Who
SERVE

ISBN 1-58334-143-9

Printed in the United States of America
Page Layout: *Bart Dawson*
Cover Design: *Tiffany Berry*
1 2 3 4 5 6 7 8 9 10 • 02 03 04 05 06 07 08 09 10

TABLE OF CONTENTS

Introduction....................................9

CELEBRATING...

1. Those Who Serve.......................11
2. America...............................23
3. One Nation Under God...................35
4. Courage...............................47
5. Faith.................................57
6. Service, Sacrifice, and Love...........67
7. The Struggle Over Adversity............81
8. The Struggle for Freedom and Justice....91
9. With a Spirit of Optimism.............101
10. Honor and Integrity.................111
11. With the Courage to Persevere.......121
12. The Family That Also Serves.........131
13. Those Who Have Given the Ultimate
     Sacrifice..........................141
14. Our Legacy.........................151

INTRODUCTION

"God Bless America." We have heard these three words so often since the tragedy of September 11th, and yet they still bring a stirring to our hearts. Why? Because they still ring true. God has richly blessed America and its freedom-loving people. But, we live in a dangerous world where freedom and safety must never be taken for granted. The American Dream was built—and continues to be built—by the courageous men and women who serve, protect, and heal their fellow citizens. This book celebrates those who serve.

This book also recognizes the fact that America is a God-fearing nation. From the beginning, Americans have worshiped God fervently and unapologetically. And, a vast majority of Americans have claimed the Holy Bible—both Old Testament and New—as their guidebook for life here on earth and for life eternal. This text includes numerous verses from the Bible with the clear intention that Christian readers will be blessed by God's Holy Word.

The grand experiment of American democracy has, on countless occasions, been tested by forces that have sought to destroy it. In the beginning, Christian men with familiar names like Washington and Franklin patched together a fledgling nation. Less than a hundred years later, it divided against itself in a terrible conflict that claimed the lives of more of its young men than all other American wars combined. But America survived.

In the beginning years of the 20th century, the winds of war blew hot and fierce across the European continent. The War to End All Wars brought worldwide carnage, but it didn't end war. A generation after World War I, on a sunny December morning in 1941, Old Glory was dealt a staggering blow at Pearl Harbor, but the brave sons and daughters of America rose up as one and saved not only their nation but also the world.

In far-away places like Korea and Vietnam, in distant lands that many can scarcely name, America's best and bravest have carried the banner of freedom, fought for it, and sometimes died for it. And, they continue to do so today.

This book pays tribute to those who protect the American dream. These dedicated men and women serve in a variety of ways: police, firefighting, military, and health care, to name a few. Sometimes, their service takes them thousands of miles from home, and sometimes they're right next door. But wherever they happen to be, however they choose to serve, we, as grateful Americans, thank them.

On September 11th in the year 2001, America was once again tested by forces that would seek to destroy her. As before, this generation of Americans stands ready to look evil squarely in the eye and defend the precious liberties that are the legacy of our forefathers. Because of those who serve us and protect us, the Dream will live. God bless America, and God bless those who serve.

1

CELEBRATING

Those Who Serve

Your attitude should be the same
as that of Christ Jesus...taking
the very nature of a servant.

Philippians 2:5,7 NIV

And so, my fellow Americans,
ask not what your country
can do for you; ask what you
can do for your country.

John F. Kennedy

The American dream is alive and well because of those who serve us and protect us. America owes its undying gratitude to the men and women who serve in the military, in government, in law enforcement, in health care, and in the helping professions. Without them, the promise of this great nation would remain unfulfilled.

Since its earliest days, America has truly been "one nation, under God." And, the Word of God instructs us that service to others is one way of fulfilling His purpose here on earth. Romans 12: 10 reminds us, "Be devoted to one another in brotherly love." Thankfully, Americans of every generation have heeded these words.

If you have chosen a life of service, please accept the profound thanks of grateful Americans everywhere. And above all, keep up the good work...Uncle Sam *still* needs you!

The individual owes the exercise of
all his faculties to the service of his country.

John Quincy Adams

In God's family, there is to be one great body
of people: servants. In fact, that's the way
to the top in his kingdom.

Chuck Swindoll

And he sat down, and called the twelve,
and saith unto them, If any man
desire to be first, the same shall be last of all,
and servant of all.

Mark 9:35 KJV

Everybody can be great because
anybody can serve.

Martin Luther King, Jr.

Do things for others and you'll find
your self-consciousness evaporating like
morning dew on a Missouri cornfield in July.
Dale Carnegie

Speak up for those who cannot speak
for themselves, for the rights of
all who are destitute.
Proverbs 31:8 NIV

The care of human life and happiness,
and not their destruction, is the first and
only legitimate object of good government.
Thomas Jefferson

No man who continues to add something
to the material, intellectual, and moral
well-being of the place in which he lives
is ever left long without proper reward.
Booker T. Washington

A nation is formed by
the willingness of each of us
to share in the responsibility
for upholding the common good.

Barbara Jordan

There are times when we are called to love,
expecting nothing in return. There are times
when we are called to give money to people
who will never say thanks, to forgive those
who won't forgive us, to come early and
stay late when no one else notices.

Max Lucado

Therefore, since we receive a kingdom which
cannot be shaken, let us show gratitude,
by which we may offer to God an acceptable
service with reverence and awe....

Hebrews 12:28 NASB

Some people give time, some give money,
some their skills and connections,
some literally give their life's blood.
But everyone has something to give.

Barbara Bush

Service makes men and women competent.

Lyman Abbott

Speak [Lord], for your servant is listening.
1 Samuel 3:10 NIV

A compassionate government keeps faith
with the trust of the people and
cherishes the future of their children.
Through compassion for the plight of
one individual, government fulfills
its purpose as the servant of all people.
Lyndon Baines Johnson

Make yourself necessary to somebody.
Ralph Waldo Emerson

Each of you should look
not only to your own interests,
but also to the interest of others.

Philippians 2:4 NIV

Find out where you can render a service;
then render it. The rest is up to the Lord.

S. S. Kresge

Before the judgment seat of Christ,
my service will not be judged by how much
I have done but by how much
of me there is in it.

A. W. Tozer

Suppose a brother or a sister is without clothes
and daily food. If one of you says to him,
"Go, I wish you well; keep warm and well fed,"
but does nothing about his physical needs,
what good is it?

James 2:15-16 NIV

I look upon the whole world
as my fatherland. I look upon true
patriotism as the brotherhood of man
and the service of all to all.

Helen Keller

A life of service is pleasing to God. The words of Galatians 6:2 remind us to, "Carry each other's burdens, and in this way you will fulfill the law of Christ." And, the words of Jesus are equally clear: "The greatest among you will be your servant. For whoever exalts himself will be humbled, and whoever humbles himself will be exalted" (Matthew 23:10-11 NIV). But, as weak human beings, we sometimes fail to carry each other's burdens, and we sometimes forsake the path of humility by glorifying our own accomplishments. As believers, we must not yield to the temptations of pride and selfishness. Instead, we must follow in the footsteps of our Savior by serving others willingly, faithfully, courageously, and humbly.

CELEBRATING
America

Blessed is the nation
whose God is the LORD.

Psalm 33:12 NIV

America is much more than a geographical fact. It is a political and moral fact, the first community in which men set out in principle to institutionalize freedom, responsible government, and human equality.

Adlai E. Stevenson

America...so much can be said about her: The world's great superpower. The land of opportunity. A grand experiment in democracy. The land of the free...the home of the brave. And, of course, for those of us who are blessed to live here, the greatest nation on earth.

Thomas Jefferson spoke for Americans of every generation when he observed, "I do believe that America shall continue to grow, to multiply, and to prosper until we exhibit an association powerful, wise, and happy beyond what has yet been seen by men." But, America cannot continue to grow and prosper without the sweat and sacrifice of its citizens. Today, as grateful members of *this* generation, we must do our part to ensure that America, *our* America, remains the world's preeminent model of freedom and opportunity for all.

Americans believe in the dignity and strength
of common human nature and therefore in
democracy and its ultimate triumph.

Charles W. Eliot

You know that being an American is
more than a matter of where your parents
came from. It is a belief that all men
are created free and equal and that everyone
deserves an even break. It is a respect for the
dignity of all men and women without regard
to race, creed, or color. That is our creed.

Harry S. Truman

America is never wholly herself unless
she is engaged in high moral principle.

George W. Bush

May the sun in his course visit no land
more free, more happy, more lovely,
than this our own country.
Daniel Webster

America is best described by one word,
freedom.
Dwight D. Eisenhower

The land of the free,
and the home of the brave.
Francis Scott Key

Exercise your freedom by serving God,
not by breaking rules. Treat everyone you meet
with dignity. Love your spiritual family.
Revere God. Respect the government.
1 Peter 2:16-17 MSG

Sometimes people call me an idealist.
Well, that is the way I know I am an American.
America is the only idealistic nation
in the world.

Woodrow Wilson

America means opportunity, freedom, power.

Ralph Waldo Emerson

America is essentially a dream, a dream
as yet unfulfilled. It is a dream of a land
where men of all races, of all nationalities
and of all creeds can live together as brothers.

Martin Luther King, Jr.

No eye has seen, no ear has heard,
no mind has conceived what God
has prepared for those who love him.

1 Corinthians 2:9 NIV

What's right about America is that although
we have a mess of problems, we have a great
capacity, intellect and resources to do
something about them.

Henry Ford

There is nothing wrong with America that
the faith, love of freedom, intelligence, and
energy of her citizens cannot cure.

Dwight D. Eisenhower

Double, no triple our troubles and
we'd still be better off than
any other people on earth.

Ronald Reagan

America was not built on fear.
America was built on courage,
on imagination and an unbeatable
determination to do the job at hand.

Harry S. Truman

Make the Master proud of you by being good citizens. Respect the authorities, whatever their level; they are God's emissaries for keeping order.

1 Peter 2:13-14 MSG

I sometimes think that the saving grace of
America lies in the fact that the overwhelming
majority of Americans are possessed of
two great qualities: a sense of humor and
a sense of proportion.

Franklin D. Roosevelt

If you take advantage of everything America
has to offer, there's nothing
you can't accomplish.

Geraldine Ferraro

We become not a melting pot but
a beautiful mosaic. Different people,
different beliefs, different yearnings,
different hopes, different dreams.

Jimmy Carter

For this is what America is all about.
It is the uncrossed desert and the unclimbed
ridge. It is the star that is not reached and
the harvest that's sleeping in the ground.

Lyndon Baines Johnson

In democracy, the individual not only enjoys
the ultimate power but also carries
the ultimate responsibility.

Norman Cousins

We, here in America, hold in our hands
the hope of the world.

Theodore Roosevelt

America lives in the heart of every man
everywhere who wishes to find a region
where he will be free to work out
his destiny as he chooses.

Woodrow Wilson

O America, because you build for mankind
I build for you.

Walt Whitman

${Y}$ou are the light of the world.

Matthew 5:14 NIV

Novelist Thomas Wolfe described America as "This fabulous country, the place where miracles not only happen, but where they happen all the time." Thankfully, the American dream is still alive and well, and miracles still happen here every day.

Do you have a dream? America is the place to make it come true. Do you have a song in your heart? Step up on stage and sing it here. Do you have a story to tell? Write it. A business idea? Be like Henry Ford and Walt Disney: start your business in the garage. If your idea is good enough, and if you work hard enough, you will succeed because America remains a land of miraculous possibilities.

We Americans are blessed beyond measure. Of course, our nation is imperfect, but it remains the least imperfect nation on earth. And, as loyal citizens, we must do our part to protect America and preserve her liberties just as surely as we work to create better lives for ourselves and our families. And now, with no further ado, let the dreaming begin...

CELEBRATING
One Nation Under God

I will make you a great nation and
I will bless you; I will make your name great,
and you will be a blessing.

Genesis 12:2 NIV

We highly resolve that this nation, under God, shall have a new birth of freedom, and that government of the people, by the people, for the people, shall not perish from the earth.

Abraham Lincoln

The words are familiar to every schoolchild: "One nation, under God...." And, if we sit down and begin counting the blessings that God has bestowed upon our nation, the list is improbably long. At the top of that list, of course, is the priceless gift of freedom: the freedom to live, vote, work, and worship without fear. God has also blessed America with unsurpassed material wealth; we are, in fact, the most prosperous nation in the history of mankind.

To those to whom much is given, much is expected, and so it is with America. We are the world's superpower, and as such, we have profound responsibilities to our own citizens and, to a lesser extent, to those who live beyond our borders. The challenges are great, and no single individual, no matter how wise, can chart the proper course for our nation. But, *we the people*—under God and respectful of His commandments—*can* join together to protect and preserve our nation and, in doing so, give protection and hope to freedom-loving people around the globe.

America has been called "the land of our fathers." May we also make it the land of our Father...and may we make the Father proud.

Every man, conducting himself as
a good citizen, and being accountable to God
alone for his religious opinions, ought to be
protected in worshiping the Deity according to
the dictates of his own conscience.

George Washington

And to the same Divine Author of every good
and perfect gift, we are indebted for
all those privileges and advantages, religious
as well as civil, which are so richly enjoyed
in this favored land.

James Madison

Either we are adrift in chaos or we are
individuals, created, loved, upheld and placed
purposefully, exactly where we are. Can you
believe that? Can you trust God for that?

Elisabeth Elliot

The Lord keeps watch over you
as you come and go, both now and forever.

Psalm 121:8 NLT

Freedom is not a gift bestowed upon us by
other men, but a right that belongs to us by
the laws of God and nature. I never doubted
the existence of the Deity, that He made
the world and governed it by his Providence.
The pleasures of this world are rather from
God's goodness than our own merit. Whoever
shall introduce into the public affairs
the principles of primitive Christianity
will change the face of the world.

Ben Franklin

We have staked the whole future of American
civilization, not upon the power of government,
far from it. We have staked the future of all of
our political institutions upon the capacity of
each and all of us to govern ourselves, to control
ourselves, to sustain ourselves according to
the Ten Commandments of God.

James Madison

O praise the LORD, all ye nations:
praise him, all ye people. For his merciful
kindness is great toward us: and the truth
of the LORD endureth for ever.
Praise ye the LORD.

Psalm 117 KJV

I shall know but one country.
The ends I aim at shall be my
country's, my God's, and Truth's.

Daniel Webster

The reason that Christianity is the best friend
of government is because Christianity is the
only religion that changes the heart.

Thomas Jefferson

Therefore, if anyone is in Christ, he is
a new creation; the old has gone,
the new has come!

2 Corinthians 5:17 NIV

The amazing thing about Jesus is
that He doesn't just patch up our lives,
He gives us a brand new sheet,
a clean slate to start over, all new.

Gloria Gaither

He is the God of wholeness and restoration.

Stormie Omartian

No people can be bound to acknowledge
and adore the Invisible Hand which conducts
the affairs of men more than the people of
the United States.

George Washington

The Almighty God has blessed our land
in many ways. He has given our people stout
hearts and strong arms with which to strike
mighty blows for freedom and truth. He has
given to our country a faith which has become
the hope of all peoples in an anguished world.

Franklin D. Roosevelt (Inaugural Address, 1945)

God is going to reveal to us things he never
revealed before *if* we put our hands in His.
No books ever go into my laboratory.
The thing I am to do and the way of doing it
are revealed to me. I never have to grope for
methods. The method is revealed to me
the moment I am inspired to create
something new. Without God to draw aside
the curtain I would be helpless.

George Washington Carver

You have rights antecedent to all earthly
governments; rights that cannot be repeated
or retrained by human laws; rights derived
from the Great Legislator of the Universe.

John Adams

It is impossible to account for the creation
of the universe without the agency of
a Supreme Being. It is impossible to govern
the universe without the aid of a Supreme
Being. It is impossible to reason without
arriving at a Supreme Being.

George Washington

We are not weak, if we make proper use
of those means which the God of nature
hath placed in our power. The battle, sir,
is not to the strong alone; it is to the vigilant,
the active, the brave.

Patrick Henry

The choice before us is plain, Christ or chaos,
conviction or compromise, discipline or
disintegration. America's future depends
upon demonstrating God's government.

Peter Marshall

Delighting thyself in the Lord is
the sudden realization that He
has become the desire of your heart.

Beth Moore

The highest glory of the American Revolution
was this; it connected in one indissoluble bond
the principles of civil government with the
principles of Christianity. From the day of
the Declaration, the American people were
bound by the laws of God....

John Quincy Adams

If we make religion our business,
God will make it our blessedness.

John Adams

The next time you're disappointed, don't panic.
Don't give up. Just be patient and
let God remind you he's still in control.

Max Lucado

Honor GOD with everything you own; give him the first and the best. Your barns will burst, your wine vats will brim over.

Proverbs 3:9-10 MSG

When we honor God and place Him at the center of our lives, every day is a cause for celebration. God fills each day to the brim with possibilities, and He challenges us to use our lives for His purposes. Every morning at dawn, the sun breaks over the Atlantic Ocean on a land of freedom and opportunity. The new day is presented to us free of charge, but we must beware: Today is a non-renewable resource—once it's gone, it's gone forever. Our responsibility—both as Americans and believers—is to use this day in the service of God's will and in the service of His people.

4

CELEBRATING

Courage

I lift up my eyes to the hills—where does my help come from? My help comes from the LORD, the Maker of heaven and earth.

Psalm 121:1-2 NIV

The only thing we have to fear
is fear itself.

Franklin D. Roosevelt

We Americans know that running away from problems only perpetuates them. We know that fear begets more fear and that anxiety is a poor counselor. As the Massachusetts-born philosopher Henry David Thoreau once observed, "Nothing is so much to be feared as fear."

In difficult times, we learn lessons that we could have learned in no other way: We learn about life, but more importantly, we learn about ourselves. Adversity visits everyone—no human being is beyond Old Man Trouble's reach. But, Old Man Trouble is not only an unwelcome guest, he is also an invaluable teacher. If we are to become mature human beings, it is our duty to learn from the inevitable hardships and heartbreaks of life.

When we trust God completely, we have every reason to live courageously. God is in His heaven, we are His children, and He is in control. May we follow His Word and seek His will, knowing that faith in the Father is the immovable cornerstone in the foundation of courageous living.

God grant me the courage not to give up
fighting for what I think is right,
even if I think it is hopeless.

Chester Nimitz

Courage is the ladder on which all
the other virtues mount.

Clare Boothe Luce

Down through the centuries, in times
of trouble and trial, God has brought courage
to the hearts of those who love Him. The Bible
is filled with assurances of God's help and
comfort in every kind of trouble which might
cause fears to arise in the human heart. You can
look ahead with promise, hope, and joy.

Billy Graham

Be strong and courageous, and do the work.
Do not be afraid or discouraged,
for the Lord God, my God, is with you.

1 Chronicles 28:20 NIV

For God hath not given us the spirit of fear;
but of power, and of love,
and of a sound mind.

2 Timothy 1:7 KJV

What is courage? It is the ability to be strong
in trust, in conviction, in obedience.
To be courageous is to step out in faith—
to trust and obey, no matter what.

Kay Arthur

Courage is doing what you're afraid to do.
There can be no courage unless you're scared.

Eddie Rickenbacker

Fill your mind with thoughts of God
rather than with thoughts of fear.

Norman Vincent Peale

You gain strength, courage and confidence
every time you look fear in the face.

Eleanor Roosevelt

If a person fears God, he or she has no reason
to fear anything else. On the other hand,
if a person does not fear God,
then fear becomes a way of life.

Beth Moore

Fear thou not; for I am with thee.

Isaiah 41:10 KJV

This will remain the home of the free
so long as it is the home of the brave.

Elmer Davis

One man with courage makes a majority.

Andrew Jackson

Fear of man will prove to be a snare, but
whoever trusts in the LORD is kept safe.

Proverbs 29:25 NIV

His hand on me is a father's hand,
gently guiding and encouraging. His hand lets
me know he is with me, so I am not afraid.

Mary Morrison Suggs

Courage is fear holding on a minute longer.

George S. Patton

I sought the LORD, and he answered me;
he delivered me from all my fears.

Psalm 34:4 NIV

Courage is contagious.

Billy Graham

America was not built on fear.
America was built on courage,
on imagination and an unbeatable
determination to do the job at hand.

Harry S. Truman

Conscience is the root of all true courage;
if a man would be brave
let him obey his conscience.

James Freeman Clarke

For without belittling the courage with which
men have died, we should not forget those acts
of courage with which men have lived.
A man does what he must in spite of
personal consequences, in spite of
obstacles and dangers and pressures, and
that is the basis of all human morality.

John F. Kennedy

Courage is rarely reckless or foolish.
Courage usually involves a highly realistic
estimate of the odds that must be faced.

Margaret Truman

Bravery is the capacity to perform properly
even when scared half to death.
Omar Bradley

Do what you fear, and
the death of fear is certain.
Ralph Waldo Emerson

You've got to be brave, and you've got
to be bold...brave enough to take your chance
on your own judgment, what's right and what's
wrong, what's good and what's bad.
Robert Frost

The LORD himself goes before you and
will be with you; he will never leave you
nor forsake you. Do not be afraid;
do not be discouraged.
Deuteronomy 31:8 NIV

As Americans living in a dangerous world, we know all too well that life is a tapestry of events: some grand, some not-so-grand, and some downright tragic. When we reach the mountaintops of life, it is easy to be courageous. But, when the storm clouds form overhead and we find ourselves in the dark valley of despair, our faith is stretched, sometimes to the breaking point. As believers, we can be comforted: Wherever we find ourselves, whether at the top of the mountain or the depths of the valley, God is there, and because He cares for us, we can live courageously.

The next time you find your courage tested to the limit, remember that God is as near as your next breath, and remember that He offers salvation to His children. He is your shield and your strength; He is your protector and your deliverer. Call upon Him in your hour of need and then be comforted. Whatever your challenge, whatever your trouble, God can handle it. And will.

5

CELEBRATING

Faith

Have faith in the LORD your God
and you will be upheld....

2 Chronicles 20:20 NIV

If fear is cultivated it will become stronger; if faith is cultivated it will achieve mastery.

John Paul Jones

★ ★ ★

On September 11, 2001, the firefighters from Ladder 6 were among the first to arrive at the North Tower. As they stood together in the lobby, preparing for an 80-story climb, they heard the sound and saw the reflection of the second explosion; the South Tower, too, had been hit. Undaunted—and with 110 pounds of gear on their backs—the six men began climbing. They made it to the 27th floor when they heard and felt a rumble like no other. At 9:50, the South Tower fell, and Battalion Chief John Jonas ordered his men to turn around and begin their descent. Jonas knew that if one tower had fallen, so, too, might the second.

The firefighters of Ladder 6 rushed down the stairs until they came upon Josephine Harris, a 60-year old woman who, having already walked down 50 flights, was exhausted. The six firefighters stayed together, helping Harris step by agonizing step. Finally, on the fourth floor, Josephine stopped completely, and the firefighters stopped right along with her. Then the building fell.

More than 100 stories of concrete and steel crashed around the firefighters of Ladder 6, but the stairwell offered protection. The firefighters *and* Josephine Harris were trapped in the rubble, but miraculously, they were all alive. How had they lived? The stairway of the North Tower, between the second and fourth floors, was left standing. And, because Josephine Harris had stopped there, the firefighters had been spared. Slowly but surely, six men and one woman emerged from the debris of the North Tower—alive.

Do you possess the faith to believe in miracles? The men of Ladder 6 certainly do. And, so should you.

Faith releases life and sets us free.
Harry Emerson Fosdick

Fight the good fight of faith; take hold of
the eternal life to which you were called....
1 Timothy 6:12 NASB

A faith that hasn't been tested can't be trusted.
Adrian Rogers

We live by faith, not by sight.
2 Corinthians 5:7 NIV

Faith ought not to be a plaything.
If we believe, we should believe like giants.
Mary McLeod Bethune

Fear knocked at the door. Faith answered.
No one was there.

Anonymous

Yes, I have doubted; I have wandered off
the path; I have been lost. But,
I have always returned; my faith
has wavered but has saved me.

Helen Hayes

Our institutions of freedom will not survive
unless they are constantly replenished
by the faith that gave them birth.

John Foster Dulles

The righteous will live by his faith.

Habakkuk 2:4 NIV

Faith is one of the forces by which men live,
and the total absence of it means collapse.

William James

I never really look for things. I accept
whatever God throws my way.
Whichever way God turns my feet, I go.

Pearl Bailey

"But David encouraged himself in the Lord
his God": and the result was a magnificent
victory in which all that they had lost was
more than restored to them. This always
will be and always must be the result of a
courageous faith, because faith lays hold of
the omnipotence of God.

Hannah Whitall Smith

Faith takes God without any ifs. If God says
anything, faith says, "I believe it";
faith says, "Amen" to it.

D. L. Moody

All I have seen teaches me to trust
the creator for all I have not seen.
Ralph Waldo Emerson

Now faith is being sure of what we hope for
and certain of what we do not see.
Hebrews 11:1 NIV

Faith is not anti-intellectual. It is an act of
man that reaches beyond
the limits of our five senses.
Billy Graham

The beautiful thing about this adventure
called faith is that we can count
on Him never to lead us astray.
Chuck Swindoll

Faith is not believing that God can,
but that God will!

Abraham Lincoln

Ours is not only a fortunate people but
a very practical people, with vision high but
with their feet on the earth, with belief
in themselves and with faith in God.

Warren G. Harding

Those who hope in the LORD
will inherit the land.

Psalm 37:9 NIV

Our faith grows by expression.
If we want to keep our faith,
we must share it. We must act.

Billy Graham

There are no hopeless situations, there are only people who have grown hopeless.

Clare Boothe Luce

Happy is he...whose hope is
in the LORD his God.

Psalm 146:5 KJV

Be hopeful! For tomorrow has
never happened before.

Robert Schuller

The only limit to our realization of tomorrow
will be our doubts of today. Let us move
forward with strong and active faith.

Franklin D. Roosevelt

When a suffering woman sought healing by merely touching the hem of His cloak, Jesus replied, "Daughter, be of good comfort; thy faith hath made thee whole" (Matthew 9:24 KJV). The message to believers is clear: if we are to be made whole by God, we must live by faith. But, when we face adversity, illness, or heartbreak, living by faith can be difficult indeed. Still, God remains faithful to us, and we should remain faithful to Him. When we do, we not only glorify the One who made us, we also become worthy examples to those whom we serve.

6

CELEBRATING

Service, Sacrifice, and Love

And the Lord make you to increase
and abound in love one toward another,
and toward all men....

1 Thessalonians 3:12 KJV

Look up and not down.
Look forward and not back.
Look out and not in,
and lend a hand.

Edward Everett Hale

Americans have been richly blessed, and they are quick to share their blessings. Whether the needs are here at home or far away, the response is the same: Americans care enough to lend a hand.

Over a century ago, novelist Herman Melville observed, "We cannot live only for ourselves. A thousand fibers connect us with our fellow men." Nothing has changed since then. The world is still a difficult place where too many people struggle for the bare necessities of life. And so we, as a prosperous people, must give generously to those who are unable to help themselves.

If you have chosen a life of service, please accept the profound thanks of a grateful nation. And then, say a prayer of thanks to the heavenly Father whose purposes you serve. God sees your good works and, in His own time and His own way, He will bless you for them.

Some people give time, some give money,
some their skills and connections,
some literally give their life's blood.
But everyone has something to give.

Barbara Bush

No race of people ever got upon its feet
without severe and constant struggle, often
in the face of the greatest disappointment.

Booker T. Washington

Let every nation know, whether it wishes us
well or ill, we shall pay any price,
bear any burden, meet any hardship,
support any friend, oppose any foe,
to assure the survival and success of liberty.

John F. Kennedy

If you do not stand firm in your faith,
you will not stand at all.

Isaiah 7:9 NIV

Am I ignitable? God deliver me from
the dread asbestos of "other things."
Saturate me with the oil of the Spirit
that I may be aflame.

Jim Elliot

Freedom! No word was ever spoken that held
out greater hope, demanded greater sacrifice,
needed more to be nurtured, blessed more
the giver, cursed more its destroyer, or come
closer to being God's will on earth.
And, I think that it is worth fighting for.

Omar Bradley

He did it with all his heart, and prospered.

2 Chronicles 31:21 KJV

I would rather be exposed to the inconveniences
attending too much liberty than
to those attending too small a degree of it.

Thomas Jefferson

We are not to expect to be translated
from despotism to liberty in a featherbed.

Thomas Jefferson

Those who hope in the LORD will renew
their strength. They will soar on wings like
eagles; they will run and not grow weary,
they will walk and not be faint.

Isaiah 40:31 NIV

Those who expect to reap the blessings of
freedom must, like men, undergo
the fatigue of supporting it.

Thomas Paine

Get absolutely enthralled with something.
Throw yourself into it with abandon.
Get out of yourself. Be somebody.
Do something.

Norman Vincent Peale

It's not difficult to make an impact on your world. All you really have to do is put the needs of others ahead of your own. You can make a difference with a little time and a big heart.

James Dobson

God loves a cheerful giver.

2 Corinthians 9:7 NIV

When you cease to make a contribution,
you begin to die.

Eleanor Roosevelt

He climbs highest who helps another up.

Zig Ziglar

Let us not become weary in doing good,
for at the proper time we will reap
a harvest if we do not give up.

Galatians 6:9 NIV

There is no happiness in having, or in getting,
but only in giving.

Henry Drummond

The Lord has abundantly blessed me all
of my life. I'm not trying to pay Him back
for all of His wonderful gifts; I just realize that
He gave them to me to give away.

Lisa Whelchel

It is one of the most beautiful compensations
of this life that no man can sincerely try
to help another without helping himself.

Ralph Waldo Emerson

Freely you have received, freely give.

Matthew 10:8 NIV

The love we give away is
the only love we keep.

Elbert Hubbard

I have decided to stick with love.
>   Hate is too great a burden to bear.
>>>   *Martin Luther King, Jr.*

You have heard that it was said,
>   "Love your neighbor and hate your enemy."
>   But I tell you: Love your enemies and
>   pray for those who persecute you.
>>>   *Matthew 5:43-44 NIV*

Hating people is like burning down
>   your own house to get rid of a rat.
>>>   *Harry Emerson Fosdick*

Joy is love exalted; peace is love in repose;
>   gentleness is love in society; goodness is love
>   in action; faith is love on the battlefield;
>   meekness is love in school; and temperance
>   is love in training.
>>>   D. L. Moody

In the presence of love, miracles happen.

Robert Schuller

If I speak with human eloquence and
    angelic ecstasy but don't love,
I'm nothing but the creaking of a rusty gate.

1 Corinthians 13:1 MSG

Love is the seed of all hope.
    It is the enticement to trust, to risk,
        to try, and to go on.

Gloria Gaither

W hat the world really needs is more love and less paperwork.

Pearl Bailey

Almost a century ago, Dale Carnegie began teaching courses on enthusiasm and salesmanship. Carnegie's classic book, *How to Win Friends and Influence People*, remains a perennial best seller, and his formula for success remains straightforward: Mr. Carnegie advised, "Become genuinely interested in other people." Ben Franklin would have agreed. Franklin observed, "A man wrapped up in himself makes a very small package." Indeed, self-absorption is not only a surefire way to shrink one's soul, it is also a proven prescription for unhappiness. But, when we look *outside* ourselves and become genuinely concerned for the well-being of others, we do them *and* ourselves an enduring service. When we become genuinely interested in other people and act accordingly, we do God's will here on earth as we follow in the footsteps of His Son.

7

CELEBRATING

The Struggle
Over Adversity

In this world you will have trouble.
But take heart! I have overcome the world.

John 16:33 NIV

It is not in the still calm of life,
or in repose of pacific station
that great characters are formed.
Great necessities call our great virtues.

Abigail Adams

Elbert Hubbard observed, "When troubles arise, wise men go to their work." Easier said than done. During difficult times, we are often tempted to complain, to worry, to blame, and to do little else. Usually, complaints and worries change nothing; intelligent work, on the other hand, changes everything for the better.

In times of danger and adversity, even the most dedicated men and women can, for a while, lose hope. We must never abandon our hopes. America was built upon the hopes and dreams of its citizens; if we are to build a better nation for our children and theirs, we must continue to believe in—and work for—a brighter future.

Undeniably, America faces serious challenges both at home and abroad. The world, it seems is an ever-more-dangerous place, and solutions seem harder than ever to come by. But, even in a dangerous world, we must not give in; we must persevere. What's required are faith, work, wisdom, courage, and teamwork. Then, when we stand united and face the dangers of the world with open eyes and courageous hearts, no adversary on earth can defeat us.

First, remember that no matter how bad
a situation is, it's not as bad as you think.

Colin Powell

We are troubled on every side, yet
not distressed; we are perplexed, but
not in despair; persecuted, but not forsaken;
cast down, but not destroyed....

2 Corinthians 4:8-9 KJV

Often, in the midst of great problems,
we stop short of the real blessing God
has for us, which is a fresh vision of who He is.

Anne Graham Lotz

God is our refuge and strength,
a very present help in trouble.

Psalm 46:1 KJV

A brook would lose its song if God
removed the rocks.

Anonymous

The roots grow deep when the winds
are strong.

Chuck Swindoll

When you go through deep waters and
great trouble, I will be with you.
When you go through the rivers of difficulty,
you will not drown! When you walk through
the fire of oppression, you will not be burned
up; the flames will not consume you.
For I am the Lord, your God....

Isaiah 43:2-3 NLT

Measure the size of the obstacles against
the size of God.

Beth Moore

The country is always stronger than
we know in our most worried moments.

E. B. White

Character is not revealed when life shows
its best side, but when it shows its worst.

Fulton J. Sheen

Although the world is full of suffering,
it is also full of overcoming it.

Helen Keller

The Lord works vindication and justice
for all who are oppressed.

Psalm 103:6 RSV

God's signs are not always
the ones we look for. We learn
in tragedy that His purposes are not
always our own. Yet the prayers of
private suffering, whether in our
homes or in this great cathedral,
are known and heard,
and understood.

George W. Bush

The lowest ebb is at the turn of the tide.

Henry Wadsworth Longfellow

Affliction comes to us, not to make us sad
but sober; not to make us sorry but wise.

Henry Ward Beecher

It is not what they take away from you
that counts. It's what you do with
what you have left.

Hubert H. Humphrey

I always tried to turn every disaster
into an opportunity.

John D. Rockefeller

Therefore everyone who hears these words of
mine and puts them into practice is like a wise
man who built his house on the rock. The rain
came down, and the winds blew and beat
against the house; yet it did not fall,
because it had its foundation on the rock.

Matthew 7:24-25 NIV

Then they cried unto the LORD in their
trouble, and he saved them out of
their distresses.

Psalm 107:13 KJV

The kingdom of God is a kingdom of
paradox where, through the ugly defeat of a
cross, a holy God is utterly glorified. Victory
comes through defeat; healing through
brokenness; finding self through losing self.

Chuck Colsen

We should not be upset when unexpected
and upsetting things happen. God, in his
wisdom, means to make something of us
which we have not yet attained, and
He is dealing with us accordingly.

J. I. Packer

Trouble is one of God's great servants
because it reminds us how much
we continually need the Lord.

Jim Cymbala

All people and all nations must face adversity. Sometimes, the scope and depth of our losses leave us breathless. But, even in our darkest moments, even when we feel discouraged and saddened beyond words, God stands ready to protect us. Psalm 147 promises, "He heals the brokenhearted, and binds their wounds" (v. 3 NASB). God keeps His promises. When we are troubled, we can call upon Him, and—in His own time and according to His own plan—He will heal us. May we, as Americans, call upon the same Source that so richly blessed our forefathers, and may we trust in the divine providence of the Father's hand.

CELEBRATING

The Struggle for
Freedom and Justice

Where the Spirit of the Lord is,
there is freedom.

2 Corinthians 3:17 NIV

Around our gift of freedom
draw the safeguards of
the righteous law.

John Greenleaf Whittier

Franklin D. Roosevelt correctly observed, "Democracy is not a static thing. It is an everlasting march." And, for Americans of this generation, the march continues. The beloved freedoms that we hold so dear are under attack both at home and abroad. The battle for liberty and justice, once reserved for faraway lands and distant shores, has been visited upon our homeland. We have no choice but to protect our freedoms with the same determination and resolve that it took to earn them.

The Pledge of Allegiance concludes with words that summarize the promise of America: "...with liberty and justice for all." But, liberty and justice are not simply words that we speak, they are privileges that we must defend. May we defend liberty at every turn, and may we proudly continue our nation's everlasting march toward a more perfect union. That march begins in the hearts and minds of freedom-loving Americans—like you.

Those who deny freedom to others deserve it
not for themselves; and, under a just God,
cannot long retain it.

Abraham Lincoln

The Spirit of the Lord is on me, because he
has anointed me to preach good news to the
poor. He has sent me to proclaim freedom for
the prisoners and recovery of sight for the blind,
to release the oppressed, to proclaim the year of
the Lord's favor.

Luke 4:18-19 NIV

We must be free not because
we claim freedom,
but because we practice it.

William Faulkner

God wants to emancipate his people;
he wants to set them free. He wants his people
to be not slaves but sons. He wants them
governed not by law but by love.

Max Lucado

And ye shall know the truth, and
the truth shall make you free.

John 8:32 KJV

The God who gave us life gave us liberty
at the same time.

Thomas Jefferson

Jesus answered, "I am the way and the truth
and the life. No one comes to
the Father except through me."

John 14:6 NIV

Freedom is the recognition that no single
person, no single authority or government
has a monopoly on truth, but that
every one of us put in this world
has been put here for a reason
and has something to offer.

Ronald Reagan

We will not be satisfied until justice rolls
down like waters and righteousness
like a mighty stream.

Martin Luther King, Jr.

The answer to injustice is not to silence
the critic but to end the injustice.

Paul Robeson

None who have always been free can
understand the terrible fascinating power
of the hope of freedom to those
who are not free.

Pearl Buck

We know the best way to enhance freedom
in other lands is to demonstrate here that our
democratic system is worthy of emulation.

Jimmy Carter

In everything set them an example by
doing what is good.

Titus 2:7 NIV

In their cry for freedom, it may truly be said,
the voice of the people is the voice of God.

Grover Cleveland

Justice, sir, is the great interest of man on earth.
It is the ligament which holds civilized beings
and civilized nations together.

Daniel Webster

I hope ever to see America among
the foremost nations in examples of
justice and tolerance.

George Washington

The friendless, the weak, the victims of
prejudice and public excitement are entitled
to the same quality of justice and fair play that
the rich, the powerful, the well-connected,
and the fellow with pull thinks he can get.

Harry S. Truman

Happy are those who deal justly with
others and always do what is right.

Psalm 106:3 NLT

Man is unjust, but God is just, and
finally justice triumphs.

Henry Wadsworth Longfellow

He has showed you, O man, what is good.
And what does the LORD require of you?
To act justly and to love mercy and to walk
humbly with your God.

Micah 6:8 NIV

Standing for right when it is unpopular
is a true test of moral character.

Margaret Chase Smith

Justice delayed is democracy denied.

Robert Kennedy

Abraham Lincoln's words still ring true: "No man is good enough to govern another man without the other's consent." But across the globe, tyranny and oppression still grip the lives of far too many innocent men, women, and children. When people anywhere are denied their freedoms, people everywhere are threatened. And so it is that American men and women must, on occasion, travel far beyond our borders to protect the lives and liberties of foreign citizens.

Perhaps you have sometimes taken America's freedoms for granted. If so, welcome to the club. In a land so richly blessed, it is easy to forget how hard our forefathers struggled to earn the blessings that we enjoy today. But we must never forget, and we must never become complacent.

In America, no man governs alone. We the people make the laws, enforce the laws, and change the laws when those laws need changing. For these liberties, we must thank those who have gone before us. And the best way to say "thank you" for our blessings is to defend them, whatever the cost.

9

CELEBRATING

With a Spirit of Optimism

I am come that they might have life,
and that they might have it more abundantly.

John 10:10 KJV

Perpetual optimism is a force multiplier.

Colin Powell

America was built by men and women who possessed mountain-moving faith: faith in themselves, faith in each other, faith in their nation, and faith in their God. In the future, America will be sustained by men and women of faith and optimism. John F. Kennedy was correct when he observed, "The American, by nature, is optimistic. He is experimental, an inventor and a builder who builds best when called upon to build greatly."

Our nation steadfastly preserves the rights of the naysayers to complain to their hearts' content, but we seldom follow them. Instead, we find leaders who can help us visualize—and realize—the possibilities of America.

Do you seek to be a leader here in the land of the free and the home of the brave? If so, be forewarned: pessimists need not apply. America was founded by optimists, built by optimists, and preserved by optimists. And, for that matter, America is populated by a people who are, by and large, optimistic to the core. We Americans can do great things precisely because we think we can. And, because we think we can, we're right.

Be hopeful! For tomorrow has
            never happened before.

Robert Schuller

I've never seen a monument erected
            to a pessimist.

Paul Harvey

I can do everything through him that
            gives me strength.

Philippians 4:13 NIV

Go forward confidently,
      energetically attacking problems,
      expecting favorable outcomes.

Norman Vincent Peale

The Lord is my light and my salvation;
whom shall I fear? The Lord is the strength of
my life; of whom shall I be afraid?

Psalm 27:1 KJV

Positive anything is better than
negative nothing.

Elbert Hubbard

No pessimist ever discovered the secrets of
the stars or sailed to an uncharted land, or
opened a new heaven to the human spirit.

Helen Keller

Far away in the sunshine are my highest
inspirations. I may not reach them, but
I can look up and see the beauty, believe in
them and try to follow where they lead.

Louisa May Alcott

A pessimist is one who makes difficulties of his opportunities and an optimist is one who makes opportunities of his difficulties.

Harry S. Truman

The sun shines not on us, but in us.

John Muir

Make me to hear joy and gladness....

Psalm 51:8 KJV

Optimism is the faith that leads to achievement. Nothing can be done without hope and confidence.

Helen Keller

If you think you can, you can. And if you think you can't, you're right.

Mary Kay Ash

At least ten times every day,
affirm this thought:
"I expect the best and, with God's help,
will attain the best."

Norman Vincent Peale

The more you praise and celebrate your life,
the more there is in life to celebrate.

Oprah Winfrey

Celebrate God all day, every day.
I mean, revel in him!

Philippians 4:4 MSG

Write on your heart that every day
is the best day of the year.

Ralph Waldo Emerson

The American people never carry
an umbrella. They prepare
to walk in eternal sunshine.

Alfred E. Smith

In 1919, Conrad Hilton paid $5,000 for a small Texas hotel and began acquiring more properties. Over the years, his name became synonymous with quality and service. He even purchased New York's famed Waldorf-Astoria and made it a crowned jewel in his chain. Hilton's advice for life was as expansive as Texas. He said, "Think big. Act big. Dream big."

If you've been plagued by pessimism and doubt, it's time to reconsider. Good things *do* happen to good people, but the best things are usually reserved for those who expect the best and plan for it. So, put the self-fulfilling prophecy to work for you: start dreaming in Technicolor. Think optimistically about your world and your life. And, remember that since dreams often do come true, you might as well make your dreams Texas-sized. Just like Conrad Hilton.

CELEBRATING

Honor and Integrity

Righteousness exalts a nation.

Proverbs 14:34 NIV

In matters of style, swim with
the current; in matters of principle,
stand like a rock.

Thomas Jefferson

Helen Keller could have been speaking about this generation when she observed, "Character cannot be developed in ease and quiet. Only through trial and suffering is the soul strengthened." At the turn of the new millennium, today's world is filled to the brim, or so it seems, with enough trials and suffering to last until the *next* millennium.

In trying times, we may be tempted to take shortcuts. But, as Beverly Sills reminds us, "There are no shortcuts to any place worth going." When facing difficult times, what's required is character, and lots of it.

None other than the father of our country, George Washington, wrote, "The most enviable of all titles: an honest man." Mr. Washington's words prove once and for all that father indeed knows best: Character counts. It did in Washington's time, it does now, and it always will.

No amount of ability is of
   the slightest avail without honor.
                                          Andrew Carnegie

Show class, have pride, and display character.
   If you do, winning takes care of itself.
                                          Bear Bryant

Integrity is the glue that holds our way of life
   together. We must constantly strive to keep
   our integrity intact. When wealth is lost,
nothing is lost; when health is lost, something
   is lost; when character is lost, all is lost.
                                          Billy Graham

Integrity is not a given factor in everyone's life.
It is a result of self-discipline, inner trust, and
a decision to be relentlessly honest in
all situations in our lives.

John Maxwell

Maintaining your integrity in a world of
sham is no small accomplishment.

Wayne Oates

Character building begins in infancy
and ends in death.

Eleanor Roosevelt

The just man walketh in his integrity:
his children are blessed after him.

Proverbs 20:7 KJV

Today, I am going to give you two tests: one on trigonometry and one on honesty. I hope you pass them both, but if you must fail one, let it be trigonometry.

Madison Sarratt

Ability may take you to the top,
but it takes character to keep you there.
John Wooden

All sober inquirers after truth, ancient and
modern, pagan and Christian, have declared
the happiness of man, as well as his dignity,
consists in virtue.
John Adams

The integrity of the upright
shall guide them....
Proverbs 11:3 KJV

Hold yourself responsible for a higher
standard than anybody expects of you.
Never excuse yourself. Never pity yourself.
Be a hard master to yourself, and
be lenient to everybody else.
Henry Ward Beecher

Of all the properties which belong to
honorable men, not one is so highly prized
as that of character.

Henry Clay

The most enviable of all titles: an honest man.

George Washington

If the rascals knew the advantage of virtue,
they would become honest men.

Ben Franklin

And Job continued his discourse...
I will never admit you are in the right;
till I die, I will not deny my integrity.

Job 27:1,5 NIV

For when the one Great Scorer
comes to write against your name,
He marks not that you won or lost,
but how you played the game.

Grantland Rice

Character is built slowly over a lifetime. It is the sum of every right decision, every honest word, every noble thought, and every heartfelt prayer. It is forged on the anvil of honorable work and polished by the twin virtues of generosity and humility. Character is a precious thing—difficult to build but easy to tear down. As Americans who value honor and truth, we must seek to live each day with discipline, integrity, and faith. When we do, integrity becomes a habit. And God smiles upon us *and* our nation.

CELEBRATING

With the Courage
to Persevere

If God is for us, who can be against us?

Romans 8:31 NIV

When you get into a tight place
and everything goes against you,
till it seems as though you could
not hang on a minute longer,
never give up then, for that
is just the place and the time
the tide will turn.

Harriet Beecher Stowe

America was not built by quitters. Quite the contrary, the men and women who built this nation were resolute in their determination to succeed. We should be, too.

John Quincy Adams observed, "Courage and perseverance have a magical talisman, before which difficulties disappear and obstacles vanish into thin air." His words still ring true. When we attack our problems courageously—and keep attacking them courageously—our successes *seem* magical, but they are not magic—they are the result of endurance and will.

Do you seek a "magical talisman" that will help ensure that you earn the rewards you desire from life? If so, don't go looking in the local magic shop; instead look inside yourself and bring forth the inner strength to keep working even when you'd rather quit. Find the courage to stand firm in the face of adversity. Don't back up and don't back down. Because, as John Quincy Adams correctly observed, courage and perseverance have a way of making problems disappear...unless *you* disappear first.

I am only one, but still I am one; I cannot do
everything, but still I can do something;
I will not refuse to do the something I can do.

Helen Keller

All great masters are chiefly distinguished
by the power of adding a second, a third, and
perhaps a fourth step in a continuous line.
Many a man had taken the first step. With
every additional step you enhance immensely
the value of your first.

Ralph Waldo Emerson

Let us not become weary in doing good,
for at the proper time we will reap a harvest
if we do not give up.

Galatians 6:9 NIV

You need to persevere so that when you have
done the will of God, you will receive
what he has promised.

Hebrews 10:36 NIV

Stand still and refuse to retreat. Look at it
as God looks at it and draw upon
his power to hold up under the blast.

Chuck Swindoll

Our greatest weakness lies in giving up.
The most certain way to succeed is to
always try just one more time.

Thomas Edison

To get where you want to go,
you must keep on keeping on.

Norman Vincent Peale

Perseverance is a great element of success. If you only knock long enough and loud enough at the gate, you are sure to wake up somebody.

Henry Wadsworth Longfellow

If you run into a wall, don't turn around
and give up. Figure out how to climb it,
go through it, or work around it.

Michael Jordan

Let us throw off everything that hinders and
the sin that so easily entangles, and let us run
with perseverance the race marked out for us.

Hebrews 12:1 NIV

In the Bible, patience is not a passive
acceptance of circumstances. It is a courageous
perseverance in the face of suffering
and difficulty.

Warren Wiersbe

Never give up and never give in.

Hubert H. Humphrey

I do not consider myself yet to have
taken hold of it. But one thing I do:
Forgetting what is behind and straining
toward what is ahead, I press on toward
the goal to win the prize for which God
has called me heavenward in Christ Jesus.

Philippians 3:13-14 NIV

There is no chance, no destiny, no fate,
that can hinder or control the firm resolve
of a determined soul.

Ella Wheeler Wilcox

Industry, perseverance, and frugality
make fortune yield.

Ben Franklin

It takes 20 years to make an overnight success.

Eddie Cantor

I walk slowly,
but I never walk backwards.

Abraham Lincoln

Perhaps you've heard the saying "Life is a marathon, not a sprint." The same can be said for a life dedicated to serving others: like a marathon, it requires perseverance, determination, and, of course, an unending supply of energy. But sometimes, even the most dedicated public servants can find themselves exhausted by the demands of the job.

Are you tired? Ask God for strength. Are you discouraged? Believe in the possibility of a better tomorrow. Are you facing an uncertain future? Pray as if everything depended upon the Lord, and work as if everything depended upon you. And remember the words of Calvin Coolidge: "Nothing in the world can take the place of persistence. Talent will not; genius will not; education will not. Persistence and determination alone are omnipotent."

Every marathon has a finish line, and so does yours. So keep putting one foot in front of the other and don't give up. Whether you realize it or not, you're up to the challenge *if* you persevere.

12

CELEBRATING

The Family
That Also Serves

Choose you this day whom ye will serve...
as for me and my house,
we will serve the LORD.

Joshua 24:15 KJV

No nation can be destroyed
while it possesses a good home life.

Josiah Gilbert Holland

If you've chosen a life of service, whether in the military or as a civilian, whether in the government sector or the private, you know that your family pays a price for the sacrifices you make. If you work extended hours, your family feels your absence. If you travel far from home, your family waits anxiously for your return. If you place your life in danger, your family wonders and worries... constantly.

On the pages that follow, we pay tribute to the women and the men and the boys and the girls who keep the home fires burning at *your* house. A grateful nation also celebrates the family because families also serve.

Whatever the times, one thing will never
change: Fathers and mothers, if you have
children, they must come first. Your success as
a family, our success as a society, depends not
on what happens in the White House,
but on what happens inside your house.

Barbara Bush

It takes a heap of living in a house
to make it home.

Edgar A. Guest

...these should learn first of all to put their
religion into practice by caring
for their own family....

1 Timothy 5:4 NIV

Money can build or buy a house.
Add love to that, and you have a home.
Add God to that, and you have a temple.
You have "a little colony of
the kingdom of heaven."

Anne Ortland

We must strengthen our commitment to
model strong families ourselves, to live by
godly priorities in a culture where self so often
supersedes commitment to others. And,
as we not only model but assertively reach
out to help others, we must realize that even
huge societal problems are solved
one person at a time.

Chuck Colson

Home, in one form or another,
is the great objective of life.

Josiah Gilbert Holland

When you look at your life,
the greatest happiness is family business.

Joyce Brothers

Keep your family from the abominable
practice of backbiting.

The Old Farmer's Almanac, 1811

You have to love a nation that celebrates its independence every July 4, not with a parade of guns, tanks, and soldiers who file by the White House in a show of strength and muscle, but with family picnics where kids throw Frisbees, the potato salad gets iffy, and the flies die from happiness. You may think you have overeaten, but it is patriotism.

Erma Bombeck

The happiest moments of my life have been
spent in the bosom of my family.

Thomas Jefferson

The only true source of meaning in life is
found in love for God and his son
Jesus Christ, and love for mankind,
beginning with our own families.

James Dobson

Apart from religious influence, the family is
the most important influence of society.

Billy Graham

Every kingdom divided against itself will be
ruined, and every city or household divided
against itself will not stand.

Matthew 12:25 NIV

Having family responsibilities and concerns just has to make you a more understanding person.

Sandra Day O'Connor

The family. We are a strange little band of characters trudging through life sharing diseases, toothpaste, coveting one another's desserts, hiding shampoo, borrowing money, locking each other out of rooms, loving, laughing, defending, and trying to figure out the common thread that bound us all together.

Erma Bombeck

A family ought to be a lot more than a collection of mutual needs. It ought to be fun.

Art Linkletter

A home is a place where we find direction.

Gigi Graham Tchividjian

He blesses the home of
the righteous.

Proverbs 3:33 NIV

In a letter to his beloved wife, Martha, George Washington wrote, "I should enjoy more real happiness in one month with you at home than I have the most distant prospect of finding abroad, if my stay were to be seven times seven years." Americans agree. Home is not only where the heart is; it is also where the happiness is.

Your family is your most prized earthly possession; it is a priceless gift from God. Treasure it and protect it. That little band of men, women, kids, and babies is a priceless treasure on temporary loan from the Father above. Give thanks to the Giver for the gift of family...and act accordingly.

13

CELEBRATING

Those Who Have Given
the Ultimate Sacrifice

Greater love has no one than this,
that he lay down his life for his friends.

John 15:13 NIV

I know not what course others
may take, but as for me,
give me liberty or give me death.

Patrick Henry

The fight for our freedom is not a dress rehearsal; it takes place in a real world with real enemies and real dangers. In the struggle to protect our families and preserve our liberties, some men and women must pay the ultimate price. The United States of America owes its greatest debt to these heroes.

At the National Cathedral, on September 14, 2001, George W. Bush spoke these words: "As we have been assured, neither death nor life, not angels nor principalities nor powers, not things present nor things to come, nor height nor depth, can separate us from God's love. May he bless the souls of the departed. May He comfort our own. And may He always guide our country. God bless America."

To those of us who are left behind, even the most heartfelt words of consolation may ring hollow. But, the fact remains that Americans who give their lives in the service of their fellow citizens are heroes of the first order. May God give them eternal peace, and may we keep their memories alive in our hearts today and forevermore.

We have enjoyed so much freedom
for so long that we are perhaps in danger of
forgetting how much blood it cost
to establish the Bill of Rights.

Felix Frankfurter

Freedom is still expensive. It still costs money.
It still costs blood. It still calls for courage
and endurance, not only in soldiers,
but in every man and woman who is free
and who is determined to remain free.

Harry S. Truman

I have fought the good fight,
I have finished the race,
I have kept the faith.

2 Timothy 4:7 NIV

HERE RESTS IN HONORED GLORY AN AMERICAN SOLDIER KNOWN BUT TO GOD.

*Inscription on the Tomb of the Unknown Soldier
at Arlington National Cemetery*

If it be the pleasure of Heaven that my country
shall require the poor offering of my life,
the victim shall be ready, at the appointed
hour of sacrifice, come when that hour may.
But while I do live, let me have
a country that is free.

John Adams

Though I walk through the valley of
the shadow of death, I will fear no evil:
for thou art with me.

Psalm 23:4 KJV

Democracy is never a final achievement.
It is a call to untiring effort, to continual
sacrifice and to the willingness, if necessary,
to die in its defense.

John F. Kennedy

TO THE MEMORY OF
THE GALLANT MEN HERE,
ENTOMBED. AND THEIR
SHIPMATES WHO GAVE THEIR
LIVES IN ACTION ON
DECEMBER 7, 1941.

Inscription on U.S.S. Arizona Memorial, Pearl Harbor

The cost of freedom is always high,
   but Americans have always paid it.

John F. Kennedy

War drew us from our homeland in
   the sunlit springtime of our youth.
Those who did not come back alive remain
in perpetual springtime—forever young.
And a part of them is with us always.

Anonymous

I pray that our Heavenly Father may assuage
   the anguish of your bereavement, and
   leave you only the cherished memory of
the loved and lost, and the solemn pride that
   must be yours, to have laid so costly
   a sacrifice upon the altar of Freedom.

Abraham Lincoln

Uncommon Valor was a Common Virtue.
Fleet Adm. Chester W. Nimitz
Inscription on Iwo Jima Memorial

We must be ready to dare all for our country.
For history does not long entrust the care of
freedom to the weak or the timid.
Dwight D. Eisenhower

Those who won our independence believed
liberty to be the secret of happiness and
courage to be the secret of liberty.
Louis D. Brandeis

This will remain the land of the free only
so long as it is the home of the brave.
Elmer Davis

Blessed are they that mourn,
for they will be comforted.

Matthew 5:4 NIV

CELEBRATING

Our Legacy

"My son," the father said, "you are always with me, and everything I have is yours."

Luke 15:31 NIV

Children are our most valuable
natural resource.

Herbert Hoover

Thomas Paine observed, "If there must be trouble, let it be in my day, that my child may have peace." Parents of every generation agree. As protectors of the next generation, we live as much for our children and grandchildren as we do for ourselves. If troubles must be visited upon our land, we, as responsible adults, must meet those troubles now with all the strength we can muster. To do otherwise is unthinkable.

Jimmy Carter observed, "Many of the most highly publicized events of my presidency are not nearly as memorable or significant in my life as fishing with my daddy." Those of us who, like Mr. Carter, possess happy memories of parents and grandparents owe a profound debt to those who have gone before. We repay that debt, not to our forefathers, but to our children. May God give us the strength to repay it in full.

A baby is God's opinion that life
should go on.

Carl Sandburg

We need to teach the next generation of
children from Day One that they are
responsible for their lives. Mankind's
greatest gift, also its greatest curse,
is that we have free choice. We can make our
choices built from love or from fear.

Elizabeth Kübler-Ross

Each child is an adventure into a better life—
an opportunity to change the old pattern
and make it new.

Hubert H. Humphrey

Be careful with truth towards children;
to a child, the parent or teacher is
the representative of justice.

Margaret Fuller

Our children do not follow our words
but our actions.

James Baldwin

The Creator has given to us the awesome
responsibility of representing him to our
children. Our heavenly Father is a God of
unlimited love, and our children must become
acquainted with his mercy and tenderness
through our own love toward them.

James Dobson

Children miss nothing in sizing up their
parents. If you are only half convinced of your
beliefs, they will quickly discern that fact. Any
ethical weak spot, any indecision on your part,
will be incorporated and then magnified in
your sons and daughters. Their faith or
faithlessness will be a reflection of our own.

James Dobson

I have set you an example that you should do
as I have done for you.

John 13:15 NIV

Our reliance is in the love of liberty.
Our defense is in the preservation of the spirit
which prizes liberty as the heritage of all men,
in all lands, everywhere.

Abraham Lincoln

We take the stars from heaven, the red from
our mother country, separating it by white
stripes, thus showing that we have separated
from her, and the white stripes shall go down
to posterity, representing our liberty.

George Washington

We need an America with the wisdom of
experience. But we must not let
America grow old in Spirit.

Hubert H. Humphrey

Teach [My words] to your children, talking about them when you sit at home and when you walk along the road, when you lie down and when you get up. Write them on the doorframes of your houses and on your gates, so that your days and the days of your children may be many in the land that the LORD swore to give your forefathers.

Deuteronomy 11:19-21 NIV

"The American Dream": this is a phrase that is unique to the nation we call home. Nowhere do we hear the phrase, "The Russian Dream," even though Russia is a nation struggling to become a working democracy. We don't talk about the "Chinese Dream," the "Mexican Dream," the "Indian Dream," or the "French Dream." In many places around the globe, democracies rule, but no place on earth is like America. No nation offers more opportunities and more personal freedoms, no nation offers more possibilities and more fresh starts than the good old USA. America is a land tailor-made for dreamers, especially those willing to work for their dreams.

Americans of this generation have a grand opportunity: we can leave an enduring legacy to our children. That legacy, of course, is a nation strong and free, and we, as protectors of liberty's flame, must do our utmost to leave to the next generation a better nation than the one we received from the last. May our legacy be worthy of those who sacrificed so much to ensure that the Dream will never die. And may God Bless America forever.

The LORD bless thee,
and keep thee:
The LORD make his face
shine upon thee,
and be gracious unto thee.

Numbers 6:24-25 KJV